AMAGING ANIMALS OF THE WORLD 3

Volume 3

Duck, Ferruginous — Glassfish, Indian

GROLIER
an imprint of
SCHOLASTIC
Scholastic Library Publishing
www.scholastic.com/librarypublishing

First published 2006 by Grolier, an imprint of Scholastic Library Publishing

For information address the publisher: Grolier, Scholastic Library Publishing
90 Old Sherman Turnpike
Danbury, CT 06816

10 digit: Set ISBN: 0-7172-6179–4; Volume ISBN: 0-7172-6182–4
13 digit: Set ISBN: 978-0-7172-6179–6; Volume ISBN: 978-0-7172-6182–6

Printed and bound in the U.S.A.

Library of Congress Cataloging-in-Publications Data:
Amazing animals of the world 3.
p.cm.
Includes indexes.
Contents: v. 1. Abalone, Black–Butterfly, Giant Swallowtail -- v. 2. Butterfly, Indian Leaf–Dormouse, Garden -- v. 3. Duck, Ferruginous–Glassfish, Indian -- v. 4. Glider, Sugar–Isopod, Freshwater -- v. 5. Jackal, Side-Striped–Margay -- v. 6. Markhor–Peccary, Collared -- v. 7. Pelican, Brown–Salamander, Spotted -- v. 8. Salamander, Two Lined–Spider, Barrel -- v. 9. Spider, Common House–Tuna, Albacore -- v. 10. Tunicate, Light-Bulb–Zebra, Grevy's.
ISBN 0–7172–6179–4 (set : alk. paper) -- ISBN 0–7172–6180–8 (v. 1 : alk. paper) -- ISBN 0-7172-6181–6 (v. 2 : alk. paper) -- ISBN 0-7172-6182–4 (v. 3 : alk. paper) -- ISBN 0-7172-6183–2 (v. 4 : alk. paper) -- ISBN 0-7172-6184–0 (v. 5 : alk. paper) -- ISBN 0-7172-6185–9 (v. 6 : alk. paper) -- ISBN 0-7172-6186–7 (v. 7 : alk. paper) -- ISBN 0-7172-6187–5 (v. 8 : alk. paper) -- ISBN 0-7172-6188–3 (v. 9 : alk. paper) -- ISBN 0-7172-6189–1 (v. 10 : alk.paper)
1. Animals--Juvenile literature. I. Grolier (Firm) II. Title: Amazing animals of the world three.
QL49.A455 2006
590—dc22

2006010870

About This Set

Amazing Animals of the World 3 brings you pictures of 400 exciting creatures, and important information about how and where they live.

Each page shows just one species, or individual type, of animal. They all fall into seven main categories, or groups, of animals (classes and phylums scientifically) identified on each page with an icon (picture)—amphibians, arthropods, birds, fish, mammals, other invertebrates, and reptiles. Short explanations of what these group names mean, and other terms used commonly in the set, appear on page 4 in the Glossary.

Scientists use all kinds of groupings to help them sort out the types of animals that exist today and once wandered the earth (extinct species). *Kingdoms*, *classes*, *phylums*, *genus*, and *species* are among the key words here that are also explained in the Glossary.

Where animals live is important to know as well. Each of the species in this set lives in a particular place in the world, which you can see outlined on the map on each page. And in those places, the animals tend to favor a particular habitat—an environment the animal finds suitable for life—with food, shelter, and safety from predators that might eat it. There they also find ways to coexist with other animals in the area that might eat somewhat different food, use different homes, and so on.

Each of the main habitats is named on the page and given an icon, or picture, to help you envision

it. The habitat names are further defined in the Glossary on page 4.

As well as being part of groups like species, animals fall into other categories that help us understand their lives or behavior. You will find these categories in the Glossary on page 4, where you will learn about carnivores, herbivores, and other types of animals.

And there is more information you might want about an animal—its size, diet, where it lives, and how it carries on its species—the way it creates its young. All these facts and more appear in the data boxes at the top of each page.

Finally, the set is arranged alphabetically by the most common name of the species. That puts most beetles, for example, together in a group so you can compare them easily.

But some animals' names are not so common, and they don't appear near others like them. For instance, the chamois is a kind of goat or antelope. To find animals that are similar—or to locate any species—look in the Index at the end of each book in the set (pages 45–48). It lists all animals by their various names (you will find the Giant South American River Turtle under Turtle, Giant South American River, and also under its other name—Arrau). And you will find all birds, fish, and so on gathered under their broader groupings.

Similarly, smaller like groups appear in the Set Index as well—butterflies include swallowtails and blues, for example.

2

Table of Contents
Volume 3

Glossary

Amphibians—species usually born from eggs in water or wet places, which change (metamorphose) into land animals. Frogs and salamanders are typical. They breathe through their skin mainly and have no scales.

Arctic and Antarctic—icy, cold, dry areas at the ends of the globe that lack trees but see small plants grown in thawed areas (tundra). Penguins and seals are common inhabitants.

Arthropods—animals with segmented bodies, hard outer skin, and jointed legs, such as spiders and crabs.

Birds—born from eggs, these creatures have wings and often can fly. Eagles, pigeons, and penguins are all birds, though penguins cannot fly through the air.

Carnivores—they are animals that eat other animals. Many species do eat each other sometimes, and a few eat dead animals. Lions kill their prey and eat it, while vultures clean up dead bodies of animals.

Cities, Towns, and Farms—places where people live and have built or used the land and share it with many species. Sometimes these animals live in human homes or just nearby.

Class—part or division of a phylum.

Deserts—dry, often warm areas where animals often are more active on cooler nights or near water sources. Owls, scorpions, and jack rabbits are common in American deserts.

Endangered—some animals in this set are marked as endangered because it is possible they will become extinct soon.

Extinct—these species have died out altogether for whatever reason.

Family—part of an order.

Fish—water animals (aquatic) that typically are born from eggs and breathe through gills. Trout and eels are fish, though whales and dolphins are not (they are mammals).

Forests and Mountains—places where evergreen (coniferous) and leaf-shedding (deciduous) trees are common, or that rise in elevation to make cool, separate habitats. Rain forests are different. (see Rain forests)

Fresh Water—lakes, rivers, and the like carry fresh water (unlike Oceans and Shores, where the water is salty). Fish and birds abound, as do insects, frogs, and mammals.

Genus—part of a family.

Grasslands—habitats with few trees and light rainfall. Grasslands often lie between forests and deserts, and they are home to birds, coyotes, antelope, and snakes, as well as many other kinds of animals.

Herbivores—these animals eat mainly plants. Typically they are hoofed animals (ungulates) that are common on grasslands, such as antelope or deer. Domestic (nonwild) ones are cows and horses.

Hibernators—species that live in harsh areas with very cold winters slow down their functions then and sort of sleep through the hard times.

Invertebrates—animals that lack backbones or internal skeletons. Many, such as insects and shrimp, have hard outer coverings. Clams and worms are also invertebrates.

Kingdom—the largest division of species. Commonly there are understood to be five kingdoms: animals, plants, fungi, protists, and monerans.

Mammals—these creatures usually bear live young and feed them on milk from the mother. A few lay eggs (monotremes like the platypus) or nurse young in a pouch (marsupials like opossums and kangaroos).

Migrators—some species spend different seasons in different places, moving to where more food, warmth, or safety can be found. Birds often do this, sometimes over long distances, but other types of animals also move seasonally, including fish and mammals.

Oceans and Shores—seawater is salty, often deep, and huge. In it live many fish, invertebrates, and even some mammals, such as whales. On the shore, birds and other creatures often gather.

Order—part of a class.

Phylum—part of a kingdom.

Rain forests—here huge trees grow among many other plants helped by the warm, wet environment. Thousands of species of animals also live in these rich habitats.

Reptiles—these species have scales, lungs to breathe, and lay eggs or give birth to live young. Dinosaurs are thought to have been reptiles, while today the class includes turtles, snakes, lizards, and crocodiles.

Scientific name—the genus and species name of a creature in Latin. For instance, Canis lupus is the wolf. Scientific names avoid the confusion possible with common names in any one language or across languages.

Species—a group of the same type of living thing. Part of an order.

Subspecies—a variant but quite similar part of a species.

Territorial—many animals mark out and defend a patch of ground as their home area. Birds and mammals may call quite small or quite large spots their territories.

Vertebrates—animals with backbones and skeletons under their skins

Ferruginous Duck
Aythya nyroca

Length: 16 inches
Weight: 1½ pounds
Diet: aquatic plants, insects, and other invertebrates
Home: Europe, Asia, and North Africa

Number of Eggs: 6 to 12
Order: Swans, geese, and ducks
Family: Swans, geese and ducks
Subfamily: Ducks

 Fresh Water

 Birds

The word "ferruginous" means rust-colored, and it aptly describes the head, chest, and sides of this duck. The ferruginous duck is very common in Central Eurasia and North Africa. In North America, its close relatives, the canvasback, the redhead, and the scaup, can be found.

Ducks belong to one of two groups: the divers and the dabblers. Dabblers eat only what they can catch by dunking their head under the water. Divers often vanish from view completely, as they dive through the water in search of a meal. The ferruginous duck is a true diver. It can stay underwater longer than any other duck—close to a minute. It likes to look for food among the reeds and shallow plants near the shady shore of small ponds and seldom dives deeper than 4 feet. Ferruginous ducks choose partners in March, but do not build their nests until June. A male-and-female pair build their nest together on the very edge of the shore, piecing it together out of grass, sticks, and moss. Often they make the nest so that it can be entered only from the water. This is good protection from cats, dogs, and other predators. As with all ducks, the male leaves as soon as the female has laid her eggs. The female sits on the eggs for 28 days. If she loses her eggs to a hungry animal, she can lay a new, but smaller, set. Once they have hatched, it takes the young ducks about two months to learn to fly.

Blue Duiker
Cephalophus monticola

Length: 1¾ to 3 feet
Length of Tail: 3 to 5 inches
Height at the Shoulders: 12 to 16 inches
Weight: 9 to 22 pounds
Diet: mostly plant matter

Number of Young: 1
Home: central and southern Africa
Order: Even-toed hoofed mammals
Family: Bovines

 Forests and Mountains

 Mammals

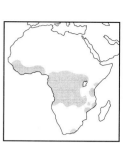

© NIGEL DENNIS / PHOTO RESEARCHERS

Few people have ever seen a blue duiker, a small antelope that lives in the dense forests of central and southern Africa. During the day, duikers rest in the deepest parts of the forest. At night, they feed mainly on leaves, grass, buds, fruit, and other plant matter. Occasionally they will feast on ants, termites, and snails. Whatever its meal, the blue duiker must be careful to avoid its enemies: leopards, wild cats, pythons, and crocodiles.

The name "duiker" comes from an Afrikaans (a Dutch language) word meaning "one who ducks." When a duiker is in danger, it usually does not run away. Instead, it ducks down and tries to hide among bushes and behind trees.

The blue duiker has two short, ringed horns on its head. While the male's horns are 1 to 4 inches long, the female's—if she has them at all—are less than 2 inches. Beneath each eye is a large scent gland. Duikers use the secretions of these glands to mark territory. They will fight to defend their territory against any other duiker.

Blue duikers live alone or in pairs. A female gives birth to one baby at a time. The baby, called a kid, weighs less than 2 pounds at birth. During the first weeks of life, it is kept well hidden in vegetation. Its reddish-brown coat helps camouflage the young duiker. When the kid is about 10 weeks old, the coat changes to the bluish-gray color seen on the adults.

Fat-Tailed Dunnart
Sminthopsis crassicaudata

Length of the Body: about 3 inches
Length of the Tail: up to 5 inches
Weight: up to 1 ounce

Diet: insects and spiders
Number of Young: up to 10
Home: Australia
Order: Marsupials
Family: Predatory marsupials

 Grasslands

 Mammals

© A.N.T. PHOTO LIBRARY / NHPA

The fat-tailed dunnart is a mouselike pouched animal, or marsupial. This creature's most distinguishing feature is its medium-sized tail—an appendage that grows especially fat when food is plentiful. In winter, when food is scarce, the dunnart lives on the fat stored in its tail. During these lean times, the creature saves energy by remaining quite still.

Fat-tailed dunnarts are common in Australia's dry woodlands and grasslands. They avoid the daytime heat by sleeping in sheltered places. Some burrow in the dirt, others nest in piles of leaves, still others hide in hollow logs. In areas where the climate is hot, the dunnarts have larger ears and tails. These enlarged body parts help the animal cool itself by exposing extra skin and blood vessels to the air.

At night, fat-tailed dunnarts become active hunters. Because they burn a lot of energy, they must consume nearly their own body weight in food every night. Unlike other dunnarts, this species does not eat birds or small mammals. Instead, it survives almost entirely on insects and spiders.

These creatures breed year round, which helps explain why they are so numerous. At birth the tiny, half-formed babies crawl into their mother's pouch. There they nurse from her nipples and complete their development. The young, called pups, emerge from the pouch after about 40 days.

Long-Crested Eagle
Lophoaetus occipitalis

Length: 19 to 22 inches
Weight: 2 to 3 pounds
Diet: rodents, lizards, snakes, frogs, and insects
Number of Eggs: 1 or 2

Home: central and southern Africa
Order: Birds of prey
Family: Vultures, buzzards, and their relatives

 Forests and Mountains

 Birds

© M. & C. DENIS-HUOT / BIOS / PETER ARNOLD, INC.

The long-crested eagle is named for the beautiful row of long black feathers on its head. This bird of prey lives mainly in forests, usually at the edge of lakes and rivers, but also is seen near farms, on trees at the edge of woods, and on telephone poles along roadsides.

During the day, this bird sits perched high above the ground, searching for birds, insects, and other prey. With its excellent eyesight, the long-crested eagle can quickly see the slightest movement on the ground. Once prey is spotted, the eagle flies swiftly downward and grabs the victim in its sharp, curved talons (claws). Then the eagle returns to the treetops to enjoy its feast with the help of a sharply hooked beak that is designed for tearing apart flesh. Long-crested eagles can be very helpful to farmers because they eat lots of rodents— even though they will occasionally steal a chicken!

Both parents participate in nestbuilding, usually choosing a site in treetops high above the ground. The nest is made of sticks and lined with green leaves and may be used for several years in a row.

The female lays one or two eggs that are white with red spots. As she incubates the eggs, her mate brings her food. It is not known how long she sits on the eggs. The babies are born with a short crest of feathers. They are ready to fly after about two months.

Martial Eagle
Polemaëtus bellicosus

Length: 30 to 34 inches
Weight: about 9 pounds
Diet: birds and mammals
Number of Eggs: 1

Home: central Africa
Order: Birds of prey
Family: Hawks and their relatives

 Grasslands

 Birds

© CLEM HAAGNER / GALLO IMAGES / CORBIS

The martial eagle's common name and its scientific name, *bellicosus*, both mean "warlike." This well describes the appearance and hunting style of this massive bird. The martial eagle is the largest and most powerful bird of prey on Africa's open savanna. Its diet consists mainly of guinea fowl, but it also preys on monkeys, hyraxes, and even small antelope. At rest, the martial eagle perches atop an acacia or other tall tree, carefully scanning the vast savanna for prey animals.

This brownish-gray eagle has a white belly speckled with dark spots. Its large and powerful legs are thickly feathered. The eagle holds its distinctive rounded head crest erect when excited. Generally the eagle is easily identified by its size, which can dwarf that of related species. It has two primary calls: a short, gulping bark and a high-pitched, ringing cry.

At the beginning of the African rainy season, mated martial eagles build massive stick nests between the forked branches of large trees. The female lays a single white egg marked with brown at the wide end. The young eagle's flight feathers are paler than its parents' and unspotted. Although the eagle's range is large, its population is sparse. Scientists are uncertain whether the eagle is rare because each pair needs a large territory in which to live (thereby crowding out other eagles), or because its population is in decline.

Short-Toed Eagle
Circaetus gallicus

Length: about 26 inches
Wingspan: about 5 feet
Weight: 3½ to 4 pounds
Diet: snakes, lizards, rats, birds, and large insects
Number of Eggs: 1 or 2

Home: Europe, northern Africa, the Middle East, and Asia
Order: Birds of prey
Family: Old World vultures, buzzards, and their relatives

 Forests and Mountains

 Birds

© JOSE B. RUIZ / NATURE PICTURE LIBRARY

This eagle's toes and feet are short, powerful, and roughly soled. All three traits enable the short-toed eagle to easily snatch reptiles from the ground. It prefers to hunt over open land, such as forest meadows, cultivated farm fields, and scrubby foothills. The eagle circles overhead in a deliberate pattern, scanning every inch of the ground below. When it spots a small animal, the eagle dives toward it at tremendous speed. Inches above the ground, the eagle pounces on its prey.

Short-toed eagles are disappearing from much of their natural range, most seriously in the Mediterranean. The problem is twofold: the encroachment of humans and the decline of snakes, the eagle's main source of food. The short-toed eagle of Europe flies south to tropical Africa in the winter. There it joins its close cousins, the black-chested harrier eagle and Beaudouin's harrier eagle.

After they mate, a pair of short-toed eagles build a flat nest of sticks at the top of a medium-sized tree. The nest is built with a deep depression in the middle, which the female lines with grass. Generally only the female warms the eggs. However, her mate is kept busy bringing her food. When the chicks hatch, both parents hunt for food. At first, they bring the chicks small chunks of meat. But before long the hatchlings are able to eat whole snakes.

American Eel
Anguilla rostrata

Length: up to 60 inches (female); 20 inches (male)
Diet: insects, fish, and frogs
Method of Reproduction: egg layer

Home: Atlantic Ocean, eastern North America, and South America
Order: Eel-like fishes
Family: Eels

 Fresh Water

 Fish

© DAVID SCHLESER / NATURE'S IMAGES / PHOTO RESEARCHERS

For all intents and purposes, American eels live to reproduce. For most of their lives, the sexes live separately in the waters of North and South America. Then, when the eels are ready to breed, a number of strange changes occur. Their eyes enlarge dramatically. They stop eating. Then the eels travel to a site in the Atlantic Ocean, where they spawn once and die.

From an egg produced by the now-dead parents emerges a transparent larva called a glass fish. The glass fish instinctively makes its way back to the waters from which its parents came. During this yearlong journey, it gradually transforms into an immature eel called an elver. On the way to its destination, an eel may even move overland, usually at night, surviving by breathing through its skin. As adults the females are considerably larger than the males. The males reach an age of 4 to 8 years, and the females an age of 7 to 12 years, before heading back to the spawning grounds to reproduce—and die.

The American eel is a rather slimy, snakelike creature with a pointed head. Its yellowish-brownish body is covered with very small scales. An eel spends much of the day hiding, emerging at night to feed on insects, fish, and other small animals. Many people consider it a delicacy that can be eaten fried, grilled, smoked, or pickled.

European Eel
Anguilla anguilla

Diet: crustaceans, mollusks, and fish
Number of Young: 10 million to 20 million
Length: 6 inches to 4 feet

Weight: ¼ to 13 pounds
Home: Europe
Order: Eels
Family: Freshwater eels

Oceans and Shores

Fish

© HANS REINHARD / BRUCE COLEMAN INC.

Although the European eel is quite common, it remained a scientific mystery for years. For centuries, people puzzled over the fact that they never saw these fish mate and produce young. So they dreamed up strange stories about the animal. The Greek philosopher Aristotle said that European eels were grown-up earthworms. In the 1700s, people believed that eels came from horsetail hair that had dropped in the water.

Scientists have now solved the mystery, or at least part of it. When a European eel is 15 years old, it travels from its home in a lake or river down to the ocean. If it cannot reach the sea by swimming, it will actually climb out of the water and slither over land for short distances. Once in the open ocean, the eel continues swimming west—for thousands of miles. It may swim for four to seven months without even stopping to eat. Finally the eel reaches a region of the Atlantic called the Sargasso Sea, where it meets with countless other European eels. Scientists still puzzle over how eels from all over Europe can reach the same spot in the Atlantic. Some say that this species has a built-in compass that tells it which direction to travel.

Once they meet, European eels mate, lay eggs, and die. The eggs turn into transparent larvae that float aimlessly across the sea. Over many months, ocean currents carry them back to Europe.

Cattle Egret
Bubulcus ibis

Length: 19 to 21 inches
Wingspan: 36 to 38 inches
Weight: up to 12 ounces
Diet: mainly insects, especially grasshoppers

Number of Eggs: 2 to 6
Home: tropical and temperate regions
Order: Stilt-legged birds
Family: Herons and bitterns

 Grasslands

 Birds

© ROGER TIDMAN / CORBIS

Hippos, rhinos, and cattle often find themselves in the company of uninvited guests—cattle egrets. These birds can often be seen riding for long distances on the backs of large, grazing mammals. As the beasts move through a field, they disturb grasshoppers and other insects. The insects jump out of the way of the cattle's large feet. Egrets spot the movement and fly down to grab the insects in their short, strong bills. Cattle egrets also eat spiders, frogs, and toads. They are not shy animals, and, in farm areas, they eagerly follow farmers who plow the fields. Cattle egrets also inhabit orchards, citrus groves, and the banks of rivers, ponds, and rice fields.

Egrets have long legs and a long neck. In flight, they hold their legs straight back, forming a neatly streamlined shape in the air. Their necks are curved in an *S* shape and tucked back against their shoulders.

During most of the year, cattle egrets are all white. But during the breeding season, they grow pale orange feathers on the tops of their heads and on their necks. These birds nest in large groups that often include other kinds of egrets and herons. Each male gathers twigs and branches that his mate uses to make the nest. The parents take turns sitting on the eggs, which hatch in about three weeks. As each chick hatches, the parents tidy up, removing the broken eggshells from the nest.

Great Egret (American Egret)
Egretta alba

Diet: small fish, frogs, crustaceans, mollusks, and other invertebrates
Number of Eggs: usually 3; occasionally up to 6

Length: 35 to 47 inches
Home: much of the world
Order: Stilt-legged birds
Family: Herons and bitterns

 Fresh Water

 Birds

© NATURFOTO HONAL / CORBIS

The home of the great egret covers one of the largest ranges of any bird. Although this dazzling white bird is often called the "American" egret, it lives on every continent of the world. But it lives only on marshes, lakes, ponds, and shallow estuaries.

The great egret is distinguished from its cousins—the little and intermediate egrets—by its stately height and the lack of a head crest. The egret's neck is especially long and thin. Its large, sharp bill is yellow for most of the year, but it turns black during the breeding season. The breeding bird also grows a "cloak" of long, wispy feathers that droop from the shoulders to the tail.

The egret captures prey either by slowly wading through shallow water or patiently standing in one place. To uncover a victim, the bird stirs the water and mud with its black feet. In spring, great egrets construct delicate twig nests in shrubs and reed beds. Both parents care for the eggs and chicks. They feed their chicks frogs, crayfish, and fish, which the parents regurgitate from their stomachs.

Early in the 20th century, great egrets were nearly wiped out by hunters, who killed them for their beautiful feathers. Like many predatory birds, the great egret has also suffered from the use of pesticides, which contaminate its food. The egret population has recovered somewhat since the insecticide DDT was banned in 1972.

Little Egret
Egretta garzetta

Length: 22 to 25 inches
Wingspan: 35 to 38 inches
Diet: fish, amphibians, insects, and other small animals
Number of Young: 3 to 5

Home: southern Europe, Madagascar, southern Asia, and eastern Australia
Order: Stilt-legged birds
Family: Herons and bitterns

 Fresh Water

 Birds

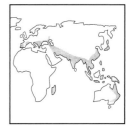

© LYNDA RICHARDSON / CORBIS

The elegant little egret is the smallest of a perfectly matched set, which includes the great white egret, *E. alba*, and the intermediate egret, *E. intermedia*. These three snow-white birds occasionally share the same marshes and lagoons. The little egret can best be distinguished during breeding season, when it grows long, dangling feathers on its back, breast, and head. After breeding season, these ornamental feathers drop off.

The little egret nests and feeds in different habitats and often flies 12 miles or more between the sites. For hunting, it prefers shallow lakes, lagoons, or gently flowing streams. For nesting and nighttime roosting, the little egret flies to the forest. A very social creature, this egret often nests together with other herons. A mated pair builds its nest in tall trees, 6 to 18 feet above the ground. Both parents share the work of warming the eggs and raising their young.

When searching for food, the little egret employs a variety of hunting techniques. Sometimes it wades slowly through the water, its head cocked to one side as it looks for fish and snails. Other times the little egret charges, splashing wildly, as it chases a frightened frog or snake. The little egret can also stand nearly motionless. Balancing on one foot, it gently stirs the water and mud, waiting for a worm or crustacean to float to the surface.

Emu
Dromaius novaehollandiae

Height: 5 to 6 feet
Weight: 65 to 100 pounds
Diet: seeds, fruit, flowers, young plant shoots, some insects and small vertebrates

Number of Eggs: 8 to 10
Home: Australia
Order: The emu
Family: The emu

 Grasslands

 Birds

© MARTIN HARVEY / CORBIS

The emu is a large, funny-looking bird that stands on long, strong legs. It looks as if it does not have any wings, but it does. However, the wings are so small that the emu cannot fly. Its body is covered with long feathers that look like hair. It has a long neck, a small head, and a short, flat beak.

The emu is well adapted to the plains where it lives. Standing tall on its long legs, the curious emu can see everything going on around it. It can run very fast—up to 40 miles per hour when in danger. In thick bushes, it becomes almost invisible because its coloration blends with the background. When it lies on the ground, its body looks like a small mound of earth.

At 2 years of age, the emu is old enough to have babies. The female chooses her partner, and the male makes the nest, usually on the ground. He sits on the eggs and raises the young. He watches over them until they are six months old. Usually, he does not leave the nest even to eat or drink. The adult emu has no enemy, except humans, but the eggs and the young are sometimes eaten by hawks or eagles.

The emu likes company and lives in small groups that travel together within a large area. Farmers once killed many emus because the birds ate the seeds that the farmers had planted. Because of this, all but one kind of emu became extinct during the 1700s.

Ensatina

Ensatina eschscholtzii

Length: 3 to 6 inches
Diet: spiders, beetles, springtails, and crickets
Home: West Coast of the United States and Canada

Number of Eggs: 7 to 25
Order: Salamanders and newts
Family: Lungless salamanders

 Forests and Mountains

 Amphibians

© KARL H. SWITAK / PHOTO RESEARCHERS

The salamander known as the ensatina is found in a variety of forms. In the northern part of its range, in British Columbia, the ensatina is brown with tiny black spots. Farther south, in the Sierra Nevada, it tends to be gray with large orange spots. In the interior of Southern California, the salamander is black with yellow bars. There are several other forms, or subspecies, of ensatina living along the West Coast of North America. They have one unique trait: a detachable tail.

When an ensatina is frightened by a predator or human, the salamander props itself up on its stiff legs and sways from side to side while waving its arched tail in the air. This instinctual movement tricks a predator into biting the salamander's plump tail, which easily snaps off. The ensatina then has a moment to escape. This "breakable" tail is fairly common among lizards. But among amphibians, it is unique to the ensatina.

In the Northwest, ensatinas live on the damp woodland floor in Douglas fir and willow forests. Near the coast, they are found among the redwoods, in chaparral brushlands, and in oak forests. When they breed in June, the male drops a packet of sperm, which the female picks up. She then wriggles under loose soil, lays her eggs, and curls around them. Young ensatinas look like miniature replicas of their parents.

Ermine
Mustela erminea

Length: 9 to 12 inches
Length of Tail: 3 to 5 inches
Weight: 1 pound
Diet: rodents, birds, insects, and fish

Number of Young: 3 to 9
Home: northern Europe, northern Asia, and Canada
Order: Carnivores
Family: Weasels and skunks

 Forests and Mountains

 Mammals

© ELIO DELLA FERRERA / NATURE PICTURE LIBRARY

Ermine hide under wood piles, in mouse tunnels, and around old barns and buildings waiting for their prey. Their favorite meals are mice, hamsters, moles, and other small rodents. They also eat birds, lizards, and insects. No matter what is on the menu, ermine usually hunt at night. This is when they are most active—moving in quick spurts, ducking behind stumps and in and out of crevices, stopping to check for food or potential danger. After spotting its prey, an ermine will watch it closely for several seconds before pouncing on it and delivering a deadly bite to the back of the neck. If an ermine is in danger, it will release an unpleasant odor to keep predators away.

Ermine can be found sleeping both above and below ground. Their nests are made of grass, moss, and twigs, or bits of hair, fur, or feathers salvaged from their prey. Seven to twelve months after mating, the female gives birth to three to nine young. Ermine are most common in areas where it snows in winter. Its coat is a dark brown in the summer. When the leaves turn in the autumn, the ermine's coat gradually changes to a snowy white with only the tip of the tail remaining black. In the spring, the reverse happens, leaving the ermine brown again for summer. In this way, the animal is always able to blend into its environment. Ermine fur was once prized for trimming royal robes and for making items of clothing, but its popularity has declined.

False Featherback (African Knifefish)
Xenomystus nigri

Diet: plant matter, insects and their larvae, crustaceans, worms, and smaller fish
Method of Reproduction: egg layer

Length: up to 8 inches
Home: Africa
Order: Bony tongues, mooneyes, and their relatives
Family: Featherbacks

 Fresh Water

 Fish

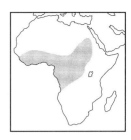

© JANE BURTON / BRUCE COLEMAN INC.

The false featherback is known in the aquarium trade as the African knifefish. Kept as a pet, this fish usually requires its own tank because it tends to fight with and eat smaller fish. False featherbacks are less aggressive when kept in large tanks, such as those in zoos and public aquariums. Their unusual appearance and interesting movements make them popular attractions.

This fish has no dorsal (back) fin, but does have a long anal (belly) fin. It swims by wriggling its body with rhythmic, wavelike movements. With this motion the fish can swim equally well both backward and forward, and can quickly retreat from a predator without turning around.

During the day, false featherbacks rest with their head pointed slightly downward. They usually remain hidden among underwater stems and thick clumps of floating plants. At night, they constantly prowl along the water's bottom, searching for small prey.

Young false featherbacks tend to swim in schools. But as adults, they become quarrelsome and prefer to live alone. Their natural habitats include large, slow-flowing tropical rivers, bogs, and pools. Often the water is so overgrown with plants that there is little dissolved oxygen. The false featherback survives in these waters by surfacing and breathing air.

Fer-de-Lance
Bothrops atrox

Length: about 6¼ feet
Diet: mainly small mammals
Home: Central and South America and the West Indies

Number of Young: up to 71
Order: Lizards and snakes
Family: Vipers and pit vipers

 Rain forests

 Reptiles

© MICHAEL & PATRICIA FOGDEN / CORBIS

On the West Indian island of Martinique, the fer-de-lance has long been known as the "evil spirit of the sugar plantation." This highly poisonous snake once lurked in large numbers in Martinique's sugarcane fields. Before there was a medical antidote, the strike of a fer-de-lance nearly always proved deadly. Even today, if this snake bites directly into a blood vessel, death comes quickly. Its venom coagulates, or "hardens," the blood. So poisonous is the fer-de-lance's venom that one woman died after washing out her husband's snakebite wound. She had some small cuts on her fingers, and the poison seeped from his wound into hers.

There are far fewer fer-de-lance in Martinique today than there once were. But the snake still thrives in the wet forests and jungles of Central and South America. The fer-de-lance's most important natural enemy is another snake, the beneficial mussurana. Mussuranas are harmless to humans. They prey on poisonous snakes by squeezing them to death and swallowing them whole.

Fer-de-lance is French for "lance iron," or "spearhead." The name refers to the snake's distinctive arrow-shaped head. The fer-de-lance is just one of several species of "lance-head" snakes in Central and South America. All of them are highly poisonous and dangerous. The female fer-de-lance is amazingly fertile, producing as many as 71 live young in each litter.

Grace Kelly Fish
Chromileptes altivelis

Length: up to 28 inches
Weight: up to 7¾ pounds
Method of Reproduction: egg layer

Diet: invertebrates and fish
Home: Indo-Pacific seas
Order: Perchlike fishes
Family: Groupers

Oceans and Shores

Fish

© DANI / JESKE / ANIMALS ANIMALS / EARTH SCENES

This humpback grouper is famous for its striking polka-dot pattern. Several were kept in the large public aquarium in Monaco, where the species is known as the Grace Kelly fish (Grace Kelly was an American actress who married Prince Rainier of Monaco). In nature the humpback grouper's spots serve as camouflage. The camouflage helps this fearsome predator hide from its prey. As the fish ages, its spots get smaller and more abundant.

Grace Kelly fish are most common near sandy coral reefs and the shallow coastal waters of the South Pacific. They are very secretive fish. Occasionally a lucky beachcomber may find one of these beauties temporarily stranded in a tidal pool at low tide. In addition to being admired for their beauty, humpback groupers are eaten by local people. They are caught with spears, hooks and lines, traps, and nets.

Like many other groupers, this species is a hermaphrodite. This means that the fish starts life as one sex and then matures into the other. Most groupers are born as females and end their lives as males. Mating in early spring, Grace Kelly fish travel to age-old spawning grounds. These gathering places are usually on the seaward side of a large reef, where there are many caves and ledges for shelter. The male and female spawn at sunset, after courting each other throughout the day. Their eggs are swept into the open ocean, where they hatch into buglike larvae. It takes a young humpback grouper four to five years to mature into an adult fish.

Jack Dempsey Fish
Cichlasoma biocellatum

Diet: plant material, insects, and other small marine animals

Method of Reproduction: egg layer

Home: Amazon River Basin (South America)

Length: up to 8 inches

Order: Perchlike fishes

Family: Cichlids

  Fresh Water

Fish

Fish collectors named this freshwater tropical fish after the famous boxer Jack Dempsey. The fish somewhat resembles an aggressive fighter, both in its quarrelsome ways and its blunt-nosed face. The Jack Dempsey fish belongs to a family of fighting fish called cichlids (pronounced "sick-lids"). Cichlids are unique in that they have one nostril on each side of their snout—not two—as do most fish.

A Jack Dempsey fish is dark blue or black, with a brilliant blue lower lip and large blue spots around its eyes and gill slits. The scales on the fish's sides sparkle with blue-green spots, and its dorsal (back) fin is bordered in red. During breeding season the male becomes even more intensely colored. Young Dempseys have seven or eight dark bands that vanish with age.

This fish has been described as "quite unmannerly in the breeding season." The males get very rough with each other when competing for females. When kept in an aquarium, Jack Dempseys are certain to dig up the bottom of their tank and tear apart plants.

Despite their rough-and-tumble ways, Jack Dempseys are caring parents. While other cichlids often eat their own young, Jack Dempseys take care of them. They also breed easily in captivity. The breeding pair require a large tank to themselves and lots of peace and quiet to raise their family.

Paradise Fish
Macropodus opercularis

Length: 2 to 3½ inches
Weight: 6 to 8 ounces
Diet: live crustaceans, algae, and dried fish food
Number of Eggs: 150 to 200

Home: Korea, China, South Vietnam, and Formosa
Order: Gilled fishes
Family: Labyrinth fishes

 Fresh Water

 Fish

© TREVOR MCDONALD / NHPA

The paradise fish is one of the world's most beautiful aquarium pets and also one of the easiest to keep. It does not mind eating dried fish food and will even keep its tank clean by gobbling up algae. Unfortunately, this otherwise perfect pet is not very sociable. It picks fights with other aquarium fish, including its own kind.

The paradise fish is a member of an unusual family called labyrinth fish. Like its relatives, it does not breathe water through its gills. Instead, it swims to the surface of the water, sticks out its head, and gulps mouthfuls of air. It pulls this air into a breathing organ in its head. This organ, called a labyrinth, acts much like a human lung—exchanging old air for new. Like a dolphin or whale, labyrinth fish will drown if they cannot reach the water's surface.

When it is time to mate, male paradise fish build floating nests out of air bubbles. The expectant father uses a foamy liquid in his mouth to glue together the bubbles he blows. He then takes his mate under the nest and turns her upside down. He will hold her there until she releases her oily eggs, which float up into the bubble nest.

The protective father will then chase the mother away from the nest, sometimes with a nasty bite. As he guards the nest, the father makes sure no eggs fall out. But once the young hatch, watch out. The male paradise fish will try to swallow them whole.

Flamefish
Apogon maculatus

Length: up to 5 inches
Diet: small fish, invertebrates, and plankton
Number of Eggs: 100 to 4,000

Home: western Atlantic Ocean
Order: Perchlike fishes
Family: Cardinalfishes

 Oceans and Shores

 Fish

© FRED MCCONNAUGHEY / PHOTO RESEARCHERS

The flamefish is one of the most beautiful members of the cardinalfish family, all of which are red. This species is recognized by its large eyes, deep orange-red color, and the two thin white lines that run along either side of its face. When young, it has several striking black markings that tend to fade with age.

On rare occasions, flamefish wander as far north as the New England coast. However, they are most common in the Caribbean Sea. There they swim around coral reefs, seawalls, piers, and oil-rig platforms. Flamefish are familiar around the world, because they are among the most popular fish in pet stores and public aquariums.

During the day, flamefish rest in shaded reef crevices and small caves or hide in burrows and empty shells. At about 7 o'clock in the evening, they emerge from hiding and hover briefly before swimming to an established feeding area, usually a sand flat. When they return home at dawn, the fish hover for 10 to 15 minutes before settling down for the day. In the Florida Keys, flamefish often rest among sea urchins. The urchin's long spines may offer some protection.

During courtship the female pursues the male aggressively. After spawning, he takes her eggs into his mouth, where he broods them. Meanwhile, the feisty female stays close to guard her mate and their eggs.

Yellow-Shafted Flicker
Colaptes auratus

Length: 12 to 14 inches
Wingspan: 18 to 21 inches
Diet: ants and other insects, fruits, berries, suet, and peanut butter

Weight: 4 to 6 ounces
Number of Eggs: 5 to 10
Home: North America
Order: Perching birds
Family: Woodcreepers

 Forests and Mountains

 Birds

© STEVE MASLOWSKI / VISUALS UNLIMITED

This familiar woodpecker gets its name from the color of the "shafts," or feather quills, beneath its wings and tail. It goes by many other names as well. In fact, at last count, this bird had more than 132 common names, including "common flicker."

The yellow-shafted flicker roams farther north than any other woodpecker—right to the edge of the Arctic tundra. All it requires is a tall tree or utility pole for roosting and nesting. Most of the year, this flicker roosts, or spends the night, in a tree hole or an empty chimney. In winter, when it needs an especially warm roost, it may drill a hole in the side of a barn or a house. In the spring, however, a very special kind of hole is

needed. This is when the male yellow-shafted flicker chooses a nesting site. He may begin digging a hole in the soft trunk of a dead tree or choose to expand an old nest. He and his mate chip away at the sides of the hole with their hard bills. The loose chips from the drilling fall to the bottom of the hole, making a soft bed on which the female lays her eggs.

In recent years the flicker population has declined throughout North America. Experts blame starlings, aggressive birds introduced from Europe. Starlings steal the flicker's nest holes. Fortunately, flickers often nest in boxes that people have carefully erected in woods, backyards, and gardens.

Crane Fly
Tipula sp.

Length: ¼ to 1 inch
Diet: algae, dead matter, and other insects
Method of Reproduction: egg layer

Wingspan: ½ to 2 inches
Home: worldwide
Order: Mosquitoes, flies, and their relatives
Family: Crane flies

 Fresh Water

 Arthropods

© BOB MARSH / PAPILIO / CORBIS

Even more widespread than human beings, crane flies are found from the Arctic to the southern tips of Africa and South America. Typically the winged adults live in low, leafy vegetation near streams and lakes. However, some inhabit open meadows and even deserts. Crane flies are easily recognized by their long body, narrow wings, and long and skinny legs.

Young, wingless crane fly larvae hatch and live in water. They can be found in nearly every aquatic habitat. The only waters that crane fly larvae do not inhabit are oceans and the deepest parts of large lakes. As they swim, the cigar-shaped larvae breathe air through tiny snorkels, or tubes, located at the back of their body. They thrive in still, shallow water, where they can easily find algae to eat.

Between the time they hatch and the time they turn into flies, the larvae change body shape four times. Before the final transformation into a winged insect, the larva encases itself in a cocoon and enters an inactive state. After 5 to 12 days, it hatches into a mature crane fly, ready to mate. A crane fly's entire life cycle, from egg to death, can be as short as six weeks or as long as four years. Crane flies living in the cold Arctic live the longest, because they mature very slowly. Those living in warmer regions mature, mate, and die the fastest.

Robber Fly
Asilus crabroniformis

Length: about 1 inch
Method of Reproduction: egg layer
Home: Eurasia and northern Africa

Diet: other insects
Order: Mosquitoes, flies, and their relatives
Family: Robber flies

 Cities, Towns, and Farms

 Arthropods

© KIM TAYLOR / BRUCE COLEMAN INC.

The robber fly might be better named the assassin fly. In the heat of midday, this tiny predator sits patiently on a stone, a stick, or a pile of dung. Any flying insect passing within 20 inches is fair game. Zeroing in on its target, the fly darts out, grabs hold, and immediately decides whether it likes what it has captured. If not, it releases its captive unharmed. But a juicy grasshopper, beetle, bee, or wasp is sure to be killed.

Many of the robber fly's victims are larger than itself, so it must use special killing techniques. First the fly takes its stunned captive back to its perch. There it bites deeply into a soft spot, such as an eye or the neck. Then the fly injects a deadly toxin that paralyzes its prey and dissolves the internal parts. Finally, the robber fly sucks its victim dry.

Robber flies are most active during July and August, when the air is abuzz with all types of insects. Although the fly eats beneficial insects, such as honeybees, it also kills many insect pests, including grasshoppers and flies.

These flies lay their eggs in piles of dung. From the eggs, wormlike larvae hatch. Scientists once thought that the larvae feed on decaying vegetable matter. They now know that the larvae are predators, just like their parents. They eat the eggs and immature young of other insects.

Spotted Flycatcher
Muscicapa striata

Length: 5½ inches
Home: Europe, Africa, and Central and southwestern Asia

Diet: insects
Number of Eggs: 4 to 6
Order: Perching birds
Family: Flycatchers

 Cities, Towns, and Farms

 Birds

© ROGER TIDMAN / CORBIS

Small and drab, the spotted flycatcher is best recognized by its patience and excellent posture. It can spend hours perched upright on a low branch or fence. When a swarm of insects wanders near, the spotted flycatcher launches into a short, jerky flight. The bird can catch dozens of insects in a matter of seconds. After a quick feast, the flycatcher returns to its perch to wait for more food.

Spotted flycatchers are solitary hunters that avoid company except during mating season. After a brief springtime courtship, the female builds a neat nest in a tree cavity, under the eave of a building, or behind a curtain of vines. The nest is usually constructed of moss, bark, and threads. The female makes it comfortable with a lining of feathers and stringy rootlets. Once the eggs are laid, both parents take turns warming them and then feeding the young. If food is plentiful and the weather mild, spotted flycatchers may raise a second brood after the first has flown.

The spotted flycatcher is also identified by its ash-colored feathers, spotted cap, and lightly streaked breast. Both sexes look alike. This flycatcher's species name, *striata*, refers to its "striated," or streaked, plumage. Its dull appearance serves as good camouflage from predators. Of all the flycatcher's many enemies, house cats probably kill more than all other predators combined.

Swift Fox
Vulpes velox

Length of the Body: 16 to 20 inches
Length of the Tail: 10 to 12 inches
Diet: small mammals, insects, and berries

Weight: 4 to 7 pounds
Number of Young: 4 to 7
Home: North America
Order: Carnivores
Family: Dogs

 Forests and Mountains

 Mammals

© ERWIN & PEGGY BAUER / ANIMALS ANIMALS / EARTH SCENES

? Endangered Animals

The swift fox earns its name from its lively manner of dashing for short distances at very high speeds. When pursued, it tries to elude its enemies by speeding away in a zigzag course. Sadly for the swift fox, it cannot run fast enough or far enough to elude hunters. Sportsmen and farmers have killed so many swift foxes that the species has entirely disappeared from many areas. One subspecies, the northern swift fox, is close to extinction. Its kin are also threatened. To make matters worse, people continue to build towns and roads through the swift fox's forest home.

You can recognize this species of fox by its especially large ears, which help improve its keen hearing. The swift fox hunts in the dark of night, listening for the sounds of grasshoppers, mice, and chipmunks scurrying through the forest meadows. It also eats insects, as well as birds that it finds nesting on the ground. It rounds off this high-protein diet with some fruits and vegetables, mostly berries and grass.

The swift fox digs its den in sandy soil or moves into a prairie-dog town after eating or chasing away its occupants. Swift foxes mate during the winter and give birth to their pups in early spring. The father fox helps feed and rear his young. Together the parents teach the young foxes how to hunt. In fall the pups leave their parents' home to establish their own territories.

Barking Tree Frog
Hyla gratiosa

Length: 2 to 2¾ inches
Diet: insects and other small invertebrates
Method of Reproduction: egg layer

Home: southeastern United States
Order: Frogs and toads
Family: Tree frogs and their relatives

Fresh Water

Amphibians

© DAVID A. NORTHCOTT / CORBIS

On a spring or summer night in the southeastern United States, a chorus like little bells rings out from coastal streams and cypress ponds. The chorus is made by male barking tree frogs. These plump, bright-green frogs gather in water to sing in a passionate chorus. When a female approaches, the male grasps her around the chest. In response, she lays a mass of eggs in the water, where the male fertilizes them.

The barking tree frog also has another call that sounds like a bark; the frog reserves this call for rainy days. In the midst of a downpour, barking tree frogs croak loudly from hidden treetop perches. While the weather remains wet and warm, the frogs spend the daylight hours in the trees. The tips of their toes end in sticky pads that serve like suction cups, allowing the frog to grasp the narrowest of branches. Barking tree frogs seldom jump; they prefer to walk slowly and carefully. Each night, they come down from the trees in search of food and water. As winter approaches, the tree frogs retreat to burrows among tree roots and clumps of weeds. They avoid times of drought in a similar manner.

A pet barking tree frog should not be disturbed during the day. In the evening, it will eagerly accept insect treats from its owner. When kept in an indoor terrarium, the frog needs plenty of water and a quiet, secluded place for sleeping.

Edible Frog
Rana esculenta

Length: 4 inches
Weight: 2 ounces
Method of Reproduction: egg layer

Diet: insects
Home: Central Europe
Order: Frogs
Family: River and lake frogs

 Fresh Water

 Amphibians

© JANE BURTON / BRUCE COLEMAN INC.

People eat many different species of frogs. However, the edible frog does have longer, meatier legs than most. So it makes a good meal…if you like this kind of food. The edible frog is more unusual in that its parents are not always of the same species. It is a hybrid, born from the mating of a pool frog (*Rana lessonae*) and a marsh frog (*Rana ridibunda*). Why would two different species mate? Frogs in general are not very picky about their partners. This is not always safe. An overfriendly poisonous frog, such as *Rana temporaria*, can kill an edible frog with its deadly skin.

Edible frogs can successfully mate with other edible frogs or with pool frogs and marsh frogs. All three combinations produce more edible frogs. Most of the time, edible frogs stay with their own kin. They are very sociable and live in large, noisy colonies. The male edible frog is a true "loudmouth." Its croak—a throaty "kroa? kroa?"—can be heard nearly a half-mile away! Edible frogs also make short croaking sounds when they are talking among themselves. One frog starts the conversation with a "kroa-kroa-knurr." Another replies with "kroa-kroa-kvairr." And then they both join in together, louder and louder: "kroa? kroa? kvairr!" After this last call, males will sometimes swim toward each other, drumming their hind legs in the water or on the mud. What are they saying? Usually the message is simple: "Go away and get your own girlfriend!"

European Common Frog
Rana temporaria

Length of the Body: 2½ to 4 inches

Diet: insects, spiders, larvae, and worms

Home: Europe

Number of Eggs: 1,000 to 2,000

Order: Frogs and toads

Family: True frogs

 Cities, Towns, and Farms

 Amphibians

© GEORGE MCCARTHY / CORBIS

Europe's most familiar frog is a small, round version of its close relative, the American bullfrog. But in contrast to its noisy American cousin, the European common frog is almost silent. Its croaks are few and far between, and the sound does not carry very far.

Of all Europe's frogs, the common frog wanders farthest from the water. Although it likes to stay damp, this frog can live on land, except during breeding season. The frog is most active on summer nights, when it can be seen hopping through woods, fields, and gardens. Some people have mixed feelings about having a common frog in their garden. The frog catches many pesky insects, such as mosquitoes. But it also eats beneficial animals such as earthworms.

In spring, common frogs head for ponds, lagoons, and marshes, where they crowd together, sometimes elbow-to-elbow. The males become so excited in their search for females that they often squeeze each other instead. When a male does find a female, he will clasp her around the waist. If she is fertile, she will lay a large mass of eggs, as many as 2,000. Soon after the adults leave the water, the eggs hatch into tadpoles.

Before the ground freezes in winter, common frogs burrow deeply into the soft soil of a garden or marsh. There they sleep through the cold weather, wakening with the warmth of spring.

Gray Foam-Nest Tree Frog
Chiromantis xerampelina

Length: 2 to 3¼ inches
Diet: mainly insects and spiders
Number of Eggs: about 150

Home: southeastern Africa
Order: Frogs and toads
Family: Old World tree frogs

 Forests and Mountains

 Amphibians

© MICHAEL & PATRICIA FOGDEN / CORBIS

The gray foam-nest tree frog looks and acts more like a tiny toad than a tree frog. To begin with, it does not live in rain forests, as do most tree frogs. Instead, like a toad, it spends its adult life in dry woods and grasslands. While most tree frogs are colorful and lively, this species is a very dull color. Like a toad, it blends well with dry mud and parched vegetation. The gray foam-nest tree frog even has small, toadlike bumps and warts covering its back. It also acts like a toad. Rather than hopping through the trees like other tree frogs, it sits in one place, day and night, waiting for an unsuspecting insect to blunder by.

But *like* other tree frogs, this species has long fingers with tiny suction cups on the tips. The sticky finger pads help the tree frog cling to leaves and branches as it climbs. The gray foam-nest tree frog even has the unique ability to pinch its fingers together to grasp a twig or other small object.

During the breeding season, gray foam-nest tree frogs travel to ponds and temporary rainpools. Perched on plants overhanging the water, the frogs blow foamy-white bubbles to create a small nest for their eggs. The tadpoles hatch just two days after the female lays her eggs. The young stay in their bubble nest for four or five days and then drop into the water below. The tadpoles must quickly grow and transform into frogs before their puddles dry into mud.

Hamilton's Frog
Leiopelma hamiltoni

Diet: insects, spiders, and small invertebrates
Home: Maud Island and Stephens Island, New Zealand

Length: up to 2 inches
Number of Eggs: up to 20
Order: Frogs and toads
Family: New Zealand leiopelmatids

  Forests and Mountains

Amphibians

? Endangered Animals

© A. N. T. IMAGE LIBRARY / NHPA / PHOTO RESEARCHERS

The rare Hamilton's frog lives in mist-shrouded forests high in the coastal mountains of Maud and Stephens islands in New Zealand. It has neither voice nor eardrums. Since these frogs cannot call to each other, it is somewhat of a mystery how they gather to mate. But mate they do, after which the female simply tucks her eggs into a damp crack in a rock or log. She then leaves the scene, while her mate stays behind to guard the clutch. When the eggs hatch, the newborn tadpoles climb onto their father's back. He carries them piggyback and carefully keeps them moist until they develop into tiny frogs.

Hamilton's frog is one of just three frog species native to New Zealand. All three are rare, but Hamilton's is the rarest. In 1942 it was believe to be extinct. But biologists rediscovered the species in a small pile of rocks on Stephens Island. Today Hamilton's frogs can be found only in two small populations.

Scientists are particularly interested in New Zealand's frogs and consider them "living fossils." Together with the tailed frog of North America, they are the only frogs in the world that possess tail-wagging muscles. Although no frogs have true tails, scientists presume that these frogs are descended from an ancient animal that did. Hamilton's frog and its two cousins may be the closest living relatives to this prehistoric frog ancestor.

Marsh Frog
Rana ridibunda

Length: up to 6 inches
Diet: invertebrates, small birds, and mammals
Number of Eggs: up to 10,000

Home: Europe, Asia, and northern Africa
Order: Frogs and toads
Family: True frogs

  Cities, Towns, and Farms

Amphibians

© HUGO WILLOCX / FOTO NATURA / MINDEN PICTURES

The marsh frog is a favorite of European schoolchildren, who often keep it as a terrarium pet. Though this species has never lived in North America, it may look quite familiar to you. Its American counterpart is our bullfrog, *Rana catesbeiana*. Both species are dirty green (about the color of an olive), with a pointy head and long, strong jumping legs. Bullfrogs and marsh frogs also share similar lifestyles: they are noisy, like to crowd together, and never venture too far from water.

Marsh frogs sometimes travel from one pond or stream to another in their search for food. But when it is time to mate, these frogs return to the pond in which they were born. During breeding season—April and May—the males join together to make a tremendous racket. The marsh frog's call is a short, laughing sound: "ke-ke-ke-ke," the creature seems to chuckle. It makes its hilarious call using two large vocal sacs at the corners of its mouth.

Like flies to honey, female marsh frogs are drawn to the male frogs' chorus. Eventually dozens upon dozens of marsh frogs crowd into a single pond. The male, using swollen pads on his arms and thumbs, grasps his female partner, squeezing her tightly. When she lays her cluster of eggs, he fertilizes them. The pair then go their separate ways, leaving a large gob of egg jelly to float in the water and hatch into tadpoles.

Mediterranean Tree Frog
Hyla meridionalis

Diet: centipedes and other insects
Home: northwestern Africa, the Canary Islands, and southern Europe

Length: 1½ to 2½ inches
Number of Eggs: 700 to 1,000
Order: Frogs and toads
Family: Tree frogs and their relatives

 Fresh Water

Amphibians

© J.C. CARTON / BRUCE COLEMAN INC.

Despite its name, the Mediterranean tree frog seems to be just as comfortable on the ground as it is in the trees. When in the trees, this slender green frog tends to walk and climb rather than hop. It has sticky pads on the tips of its toes, which it uses to keep a firm grip on wet branches and leaves. The tree frog has another special climbing adaptation: between the last two bones of each toe is a special piece of cartilage, or soft bone. This cartilage allows the frog's toe to turn all the way around while its adhesive toe pad stays stuck firmly in place.

During the day the Mediterranean tree frog hides from its predators in bushes and shrubs. It can remain perfectly still for many hours. But as soon as the sun sets, the frog transforms into a nimble and lively hunter. It often jumps out of the trees and onto the damp ground, where it searches for fat centipedes. These frogs are often abundant but difficult to catch. They can hop very quickly through the grass.

Mediterranean tree frogs always live near swamps, ponds, or slow-moving streams. In spring the adult frogs gather in the water to mate. The males have large vocal sacs that they use to call for their mates. When a male and female meet, he grasps her tightly just behind her front legs. She then releases a mass of eggs into the water, where the male fertilizes them. Tadpoles hatch from the eggs in about two weeks.

Northern Cricket Frog
Acris crepitans

Method of Reproduction: egg layer
Home: central and eastern United States
Length: ⅝ to 1½ inches

Diet: insects
Order: Frogs and toads
Family: Tree frogs and their relatives

 Fresh Water

Amphibians

© LYNDA RICHARDSON / CORBIS

The words "sweet" and "cute" are often used to describe the delightful northern cricket frog. This lively little jumper is abundant in and around sunny ponds and slow-moving streams. Although children often try to capture this attractive peeper, it is very difficult to catch. Like a grasshopper, the northern cricket frog can hop rapidly through grass or disappear into water.

The northern cricket frog is named for its call—a shrill, cricketlike clicking. In appearance, it closely resembles the southern cricket frog. Both species are tiny, rough-skinned frogs best recognized by a dark triangle between the eyes and long, dark stripes on the thighs. The northern cricket frog has a rounded snout and short legs, while its southern cousin has a pointed snout and longish legs.

Northern cricket frogs breed from April to August in the East. Those living in the West and the South breed earlier. To attract females, the males perch in shallow water and make their clicking sounds with a slow, regular rhythm. When a female approaches, the male clasps her just behind the front legs. She then lays a mass of eggs in the water as the male fertilizes them.

Cricket frogs belong to the tree frog family, but they are tree frogs that have returned to the ground. They like to bask in sunny patches of damp grass and weeds, usually in or around ponds, rivers, and lakes.

Painted Frog
Discoglossus pictus

Length: 2¼ inches to 2¾ inches

Diet: insects

Method of Reproduction: egg layer

Home: Portugal, Spain, and southern France

Order: Frogs and toads

Family: Discoglossid frogs

 Fresh Water

 Amphibians

© CHRISTOPHE VECHOT / BIOS / PETER ARNOLD, INC.

The painted frog of Europe looks much like the common North American leopard frog. But there is one big difference. While a leopard frog can snag an insect with a flick of its long tongue, the painted frog's tongue extends only ⅛th of an inch. In order to catch a fly, a painted frog must lunge at its victim with its entire body. Fortunately, painted frogs are strong, quick, and accurate jumpers. They usually live in shallow ponds and streams, avoid deep water, and rarely venture onto dry land.

Female painted frogs lay as many as six clutches of eggs each year, spaced about three weeks apart. Though each clutch contains a huge number of eggs, the mother frog lays them one by one. She deposits her eggs in a thin layer across the bottom of a pond or on the leaves of a plant. After a short while, aquatic tadpoles emerge from the eggs. They breathe through gills and keep the gills supplied with fresh, oxygen-rich water by "inhaling" the water through special holes at the front of their head. Most other species of tadpoles breathe through holes on their side. Painted-frog tadpoles swim and feed along the bottom of ponds or streams until they are big enough to metamorphose, or change, into adult frogs. They gradually lose their tails and gills at the same time as they grow legs and lungs. When metamorphosis is complete, the adult frog breathes air instead of water and swims by kicking its powerful legs instead of swishing a tail.

Red-Eyed Tree Frog
Agalychnis callidryas

Length: 2 to 3 inches
Diet: mainly insects
Number of Eggs: about 50
Home: Central America

Order: Frogs and toads
Family: Tree frogs and their relatives

 Rain forests

 Amphibians

© MICHAEL & PATRICIA FOGDEN / CORBIS

Shortly after sunset, a peeping chorus begins throughout the moist rain forests of Central America. This twilight chorus lasts only five minutes. In the silence that follows, red-eyed tree frogs climb down from their daytime perches and gather around their breeding ponds. There a new chorus begins, as the males call loudly to their mates. The females soon follow.

Considerably larger than the males, female red-eyes allow their mate to climb up on their back. Like a bareback rider, the male tree frog grasps his mate tightly around her armpits. She carries him to a suitable place for laying eggs: usually a leaf or stem directly above the water. The female carefully places her clutch of green eggs in the cup of a leaf or hangs it from a dangling vine or branch.

A tadpole develops within each egg. It hatches by wriggling until the jellylike egg pops open. If its mother chose a good spot, the tadpole will drop directly into the water. However, some end up in the dirt. Fortunately, the tadpoles have a strong, muscular tail and can wriggle and flop about on a dry surface until they reach water.

It takes nearly 80 days for the fishlike tadpole to transform into an adult red-eyed tree frog. Like most tree frogs, the adults of this species have slender limbs and long fingers with round suction cups at the tips. These frogs are designed for climbing and walking on wet branches, not for jumping.

Wallace's Flying Frog
Rhacophorus nigropalmatus

Length: about 4 inches
Diet: insects
Method of Reproduction: egg layer

Home: southeast Asia
Order: Frogs and toads
Family: Rhacophorids

 Rain forests

 Amphibians

© STEPHEN DALTON / PHOTO RESEARCHERS

On and near the faraway island of Borneo lives an unusual amphibian called Wallace's flying frog. Like other flying frogs, the Wallace's variety glides through the air to get from one tree branch to another. Its ability to fly derives from special webs of skin on its hands and feet that catch the air like small sails.

Wallace's flying frog can glide up to 50 feet across the high forest canopy. The frog makes a long, low final approach to the ground in order to slow down and make a smooth landing. Special bones help the frog snugly press the tiny suction pads on its feet and toes against the surface of a tree, giving it a firm grip for landing. In one study,

scientists watched one of the frogs launch itself from high in a tree and soar a horizontal distance of well over 23 feet!

Wallace's flying frogs have some other interesting tricks. Before mating, the female produces a fluid that she beats into a foam with her hind legs. She then lays her eggs in this bubble nest. At the same time, her mate fertilizes the eggs with his sperm. The parents then leave their bubbly nest hanging over water. When the embryos inside the eggs have developed into tadpoles, the nest falls apart. The young drop into the water and swim away. Parent frogs who choose their nesting site unwisely may lose all their young if the tadpoles fall onto dry ground.

Grant's Gazelle
Gazella granti

Height at the Shoulder: 31 to 35 inches
Weight: 100 to 175 pounds
Diet: grasses and leaves of bushes

Number of Young: 1
Home: East Africa
Order: Even-toed hoofed mammals
Family: Bovines

 Grasslands

 Mammals

© KEVIN SCHAFER / CORBIS

When a Grant's gazelle utters a loud "Kwoof!" all the other members of its herd stop grazing, raise their heads, and frantically scan their territory. A Grant's gazelle will usually sound this alarm call when it sees, smells, or hears its most fearsome predators—lions and leopards. Luckily, the gazelle has excellent eyesight and can spot a predator from a long distance. At the first sign of trouble, the gazelle will make a speedy getaway.

Like all members of the gazelle family, the Grant's species has unbranched, hollow horns, a physical characteristic shared by males (bucks) and females (does). Unlike deer antlers that are shed annually, gazelle horns are permanent. When cornered by an enemy, the gazelle attacks, using its horns as deadly weapons. The Grant's gazelle lives on scrubby, grassy plains and in semidesert areas. The creature can withstand long periods of hot weather with very little drinking water. It meets its water needs from dew or whatever green leaves it can find, a treat for which the gazelle will travel far and wide.

During the dry season, herds may contain hundreds of gazelles of both sexes. During the rainy season, however, herds are much smaller, often numbering fewer than a dozen members, and tend to be either all-male or all-female. Grant's gazelles occasionally live with other animals, most often Thomson's gazelles.

Tokay Gecko
Gekko gecko

Length: up to 14 inches
Diet: insects, small snakes, birds, and other vertebrates
Number of Eggs: 2

Home: Southeast Asia
Order: Lizards and snakes
Family: Geckos

  Cities, Towns, and Farms

 Reptiles

© CLIVE DRUETT / PAPILIO / CORBIS

In many parts of Southeast Asia, almost every house has one or two Tokay geckos in residence. People consider the geckos a sign of good luck. The "house geckos" are helpful because they eat many insect pests. Tokay geckos hunt at night, using their large eyes to see in the dim light. They are excellent climbers as well, running up walls and across ceilings—upside down! Adhesive pads on the creature's feet keep the gecko from falling. Thousands of microscopic, hairlike structures on the pads hold on to irregularities in surfaces—little holes and rough spots that may be invisible to a person.

Geckos are very vocal, using their voices more than other reptiles. There are hundreds of species of geckos. But their common name comes from the loud barking call of the male Tokay gecko, which sounds like "geck-oh" or "to-keh." The females do not make sounds, except for a hissing noise when threatened with danger.

The Tokay gecko is the largest of all geckos. It is very aggressive and quick to bite its enemies. Like other geckos, it has a fragile tail that breaks off when seized by a predator. As the predator holds the twitching tail, thinking that it has gotten hold of the entire creature, the gecko runs away. A new tail grows quickly, but it usually is not as symmetrical as the original one.

Gerenuk (Giraffe Gazelle)
Litocranius walleri

Length of the Body: up to 5⅓ feet

Length of the Tail: 10 to 14 inches

Weight: up to 110 pounds

Diet: leaves, shoots, buds, fruits, and blossoms

Number of Young: 1

Home: eastern Africa

Order: Even-toed hoofed mammals

Family: Bovines

Subfamily: True antelopes

 Grasslands

 Mammals

© CARL & ANN PURCELL / CORBIS

The gerenuk's most striking feature is its elegantly long neck, from which it gets the nickname giraffe gazelle. Like real giraffes, these gazelles use their long neck to reach tender buds and leaves growing on high branches. Gerenuk also have very long legs. A gerenuk on tiptoe with its neck outstretched can get to food beyond the reach of other gazelles. As it eats, the gerenuk may stand on its back legs, making good use of its excellent sense of balance.

Gerenuk are also remarkable for their ability to survive without water. Biologists believe that these gazelles can live their entire lives—up to 12 years—without ever actually drinking. The animal takes the moisture it needs from the plants it eats. Therefore, it is very important for a gerenuk to find plenty of juicy leaves and shoots.

Gerenuk seem to get along with one another. But unlike other gazelles, they do not form large herds. Even in crowded areas, gerenuk travel singly, in pairs, or at most in groups of 10. Each group or individual maintains its own territory. Each territory may be up to 850 acres—quite large by gazelle standards. But gerenuk seldom fight over territories. They peacefully establish their boundaries with markers made of dung piles. Like other gazelles, the gerenuk also marks its territory by rubbing its head against trees, leaving a characteristic musky odor.

Indian Glassfish
Chanda ranga

Length: up to 3¼ inches
Diet: small crustaceans and worms
Method of Reproduction: egg layer

Home: Pakistan, India, Nepal, Bangladesh, Burma, and Malaysia
Order: Perchlike fishes
Family: Snooks

 Fresh Water

 Fish

© GERARD LACZ / PETER ARNOLD, INC.

The glassfish's transparent body allows you to see its bones and organs. Most noticeable are the fish's backbone and the swim bladder near its head. Sometimes the male looks slightly golden, but that changes to a bluish-green when reflected light passes through his body. The female's semitransparent skin is a dull yellow.

Not surprisingly, the fascinating Indian glassfish is a popular aquarium pet. It needs a well-established aquarium with lots of plants, dark soil, and a sunny location. Although it is shy by nature, a pet glassfish can become quite tame. With patient coaxing from its owner, the fish will come out from among the plants to take live food.

If their aquarium is placed near an east-facing window, Indian glassfish will mate in the morning sun. The female lays four to six eggs among the underwater plants. A day later the tiny newborn hatch. At first the hatchlings cling to the plants or the sides of the aquarium. On the third or fourth day, they begin to swim. But baby beware! The parents will eat their young if the newborn are not removed from the tank.

In the wild, Indian glassfish live in fresh and slightly salty water, such as rivers, streams, and coastal estuaries. But they do not enter the open sea. In captivity, Indian glassfish must be kept in temperate water, with two or three teaspoons of sea salt mixed into each gallon of water.